Pebble® Plus

LET'S LOOK AT COUNTRIES

LET'S LOOK AT THE

UNITED STATES OF AMERICA

BY JOY FRISCH-SCHMOLL

raintree

a Capstone company — publishers for children

Raintree is an imprint of Capstone Global Library Limited, a company incorporated in England and Wales having its registered office at 264 Banbury Road, Oxford, OX2 7DY – Registered company number: 6695582

www.raintree.co.uk
myorders@raintree.co.uk

Text © Capstone Global Library Limited 2020
The moral rights of the proprietor have been asserted.

Edited by Erika L. Shores
Designed by Juliette Peters
Original illustrations © Capstone Global Library Limited 2020
Picture research by Jo Miller
Production by Kathy McColley
Originated by Capstone Global Library Ltd
Printed and bound in India

ISBN 978 1 4747 6942 6 (hardback)
ISBN 978 1 4747 6960 0 (paperback)

British Library Cataloguing in Publication Data
A full catalogue record for this book is available from the British Library.

Acknowledgements
Getty Images: Hisham Ibrahim, 17, John Fedele, 13; Newscom: Blend Images/Deborah Kolb, 11; Shutterstock: Allen.G, 8, Andreas C. Fischer, Cover Bottom, Cover Back, Artush, 9, Globe Turner, 22 (Inset), kojihirano, 21, mandritoiu, Cover Top, Mariusz S. Jurgielewicz, 6, nate, 4, Nitr, 19, Orhan Cam, 5, Patrick Tr, 7, Peter Kunasz, 22-23, 24, Songquan Deng, 1, 15, Steve Collender, Cover Middle, Stuart Monk, 3

Every effort has been made to contact copyright holders of material reproduced in this book. Any omissions will be rectified in subsequent printings if notice is given to the publisher.

All the internet addresses (URLs) given in this book were valid at the time of going to press. However, due to the dynamic nature of the internet, some addresses may have changed, or sites may have changed or ceased to exist since publication. While the author and publisher regret any inconvenience this may cause readers, no responsibility for any such changes can be accepted by either the author or the publisher

CONTENTS

Where is the United States of America?

The United States is a country in North America. It is between Canada and Mexico. The capital city is Washington, D.C.

■ **United States of America**

Washington, D.C.

From mountains to deserts

The country has mountains

in the west and east.

Prairies and hills lie in between.

The southwest has deserts.

The north is colder than the south.

In the wild

The United States has all types of wildlife. Deer, wolves and bears live in the forests. Prairie dogs and bison live on the plains. The bald eagle is the national bird.

bald eagle

bison

People

The first Americans were Native Americans.

Over time people from other countries

came to the United States.

They brought different languages

and ways of life.

At work

Most Americans work in banks,

hospitals and other service jobs.

Some work for the government.

Some workers build aeroplanes,

cars, computers or houses.

Summer celebration

The 4th of July is the country's birthday.

People have barbecues and picnics.

Marching bands play in parades.

Colourful fireworks fill the night sky.

On the field

American football is the most watched sport in the United States. People also watch basketball and baseball. Football is also popular, especially with young people. Americans call it soccer.

Time to eat

Half of Americans eat burgers,

pizza or other fast food once a week.

Potatoes, often cooked as chips, are

the most popular vegetable.

Chicken is the most popular meat.

Famous place

The Grand Canyon is in the southwest

of the United States.

It has layers of different coloured rocks.

Visitors can hike to the bottom of the canyon.

QUICK UNITED STATES OF AMERICA FACTS

United States of America flag

Name: United States of America

Capital: Washington, D.C.

Other major cities: New York City, Los Angeles, Chicago

Population: 326,625,791 (2017 estimate)

Size: 9,833,517 sq km (3,796,742 square miles)

Language: English, Spanish

Money: US dollar

GLOSSARY

fast food food from a restaurant that is made and served very quickly

government group of people who make laws, rules and decisions for a country or state

plain large, flat area of land with few trees

popular liked or enjoyed by many people

prairie large area of flat or rolling grassland with few or no trees

FIND OUT MORE

BOOKS

Animals in Danger in North America (Animals in Danger), Richard and Louise Spilsbury (Raintree, 2014)

Introducing North America (Introducing Continents), Chris Oxlade (Raintree, 2014)

United States of America (A Benjamin Blog and His Inquisitive Dog Guide), Anita Ganeri (Raintree, 2015)

WEBSITES

www.bbc.com/bitesize/articles/z49dnrd
Explore a famous US city: San Francisco.

www.dkfindout.com/uk/earth/continents/north-america
Find out more about North America.

COMPREHENSION QUESTIONS

1. Describe the different types of landforms in the United States.

2. When do Americans celebrate their country's birthday?

3. What are some popular sports in the United States?

INDEX